W9-DHH-978

DOG SELFIES

CHARLIE ELLIS

summersdale

DOG SELFIES

SUMMERSDALE PUBLISHERS LTD
46 WEST STREET
CHICHESTER
WEST SUSSEX
PO19 1RP
UK

WWW.SUMMERSDALE.COM

PRINTED AND BOUND IN CHINA

ISBN: 978-1-78685-345-5

10 9 8 7 6 5 4 3 2 1

TO...

FROM..

NAME: NORM

AGE: 2 YEARS

HOBBIES: TAKING SELFIES, KICK-STARTING THE PET SELFIE CRAZE, BEING AN INSTAGRAM STAR

#DRUNKENSELFIES

#NOREGRETS

GUYS, I DON’T KNOW... WHICH IS
MY BEST ANGLE?

EAT YOUR HEART OUT MILEY!

JUST CHILLIN' ON THE HUMAN BED.

#REBEL #PROHIBITEDPILLOWS

#HELLOLADIES

JUST TAKING A BREAK FROM
~~DIGGING UP ALL THE FLOWER BEDS~~
GARDENING.

NAME:	BAILEY
NICKNAME:	STINKY BOY!
AGE:	9 YEARS
LIKES:	CHASING BIRDS AROUND THE GARDEN
BIGGEST FEAR:	HIS STOMACH GROWLING, BECAUSE HE DOESN'T KNOW WHAT IT IS

MY FUR CAN'T HANDLE THIS HUMIDITY.

NAME: IGGY PUP

AGE: 7 YEARS

LIKES: FROZEN PEAS, AND WILL COME RUNNING AS SOON AS HE HEARS THE FREEZER DOOR OPEN!

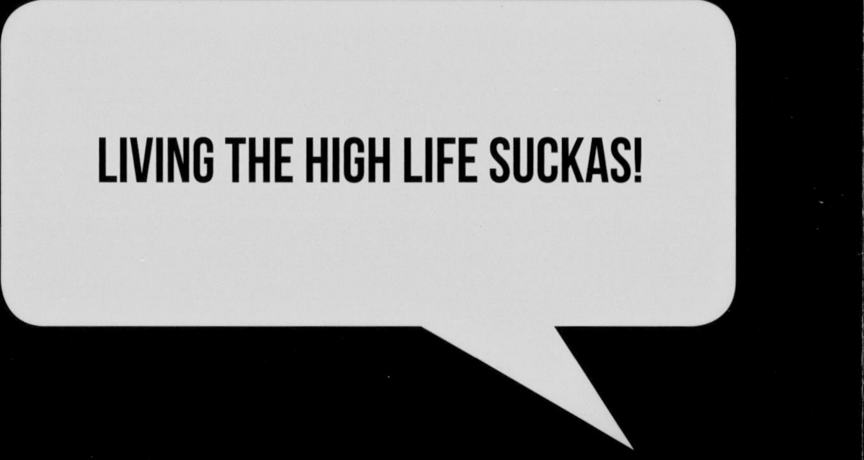
LIVING THE HIGH LIFE SUCKAS!

#ONLINEDATINGPROFILEPIC

#ALLMYOWNTEETH

NAME: BEAR

AGE: 1 YEAR

LIKES: SMILING, ADVENTURES, PLAYING WITH CATS!

IF MY DOG BED HAD A 300 THREAD COUNT MAYBE I'D LIE ON THAT INSTEAD.

#SELFIEADDICT

NAME: COMMISSARIO COLUMBEAU FORBES

NICKNAME: BEAU

LIKES: CARROTS AND ICE CREAM

QUIRKS: WAS ONCE OFFERED A JOB MODELLING DOG WEDDING OUTFITS

LOVING SOME YOGA. JUST DOING
THE DOWNWARD-FACING DOG.

#EVENWHENWEAREAPART
#WECANSHAREADOGGYBED

CAN'T DO ANYTHING WITH MY HAIR
TODAY, IT'S SO FLUFFY.

#HUMBLEBRAG

NAME:	PEPE LE PUG
AGE:	5 YEARS
LIKES:	BLUEBERRIES AND THE BEACH
DISLIKES:	BIRDS AND AEROPLANES

#SURPRISEDSELFIE

#LOVELIFE

#VAYCAY

#STAYCAY

NAME: OTTO GARSED-MILLEN

LIKES: HUMANS. SITTING ON THE HEADS OF HUMANS

DISLIKES: DOGS

QUIRKS: WEEING SITTING DOWN

WHO SAT ON IT BEST?

#ILOVERUGS

#BFF

BEEN CHOWIN' ON THOSE TEETH-
CLEANING DOGGIE BISCUITS, LOVING
MY SMILE ATM.

JUST BEEN FOR THE LONGEST RUN!
#COLLAPSEDSELFIE

#WHITEDOGWASTED

#NOMAKEUPSELFIE

NAME: HENRY

AGE: 5 YEARS

LIKES: HIS SWEET PAD AND LONG WALKS IN THE SUNSHINE

DISLIKES: SQUIRRELS

NOT TO MAKE ANYONE JEL, BUT
HAVING THE BEST SUNBATHING
WEATHER HERE.

#HAPPYFACE

#CRAZYFACE

HANK
08444 810 157*

#WALKINGLIKEHUMANS

FORGET DUCK FACE, I'M BRINGING IN DOG FACE.

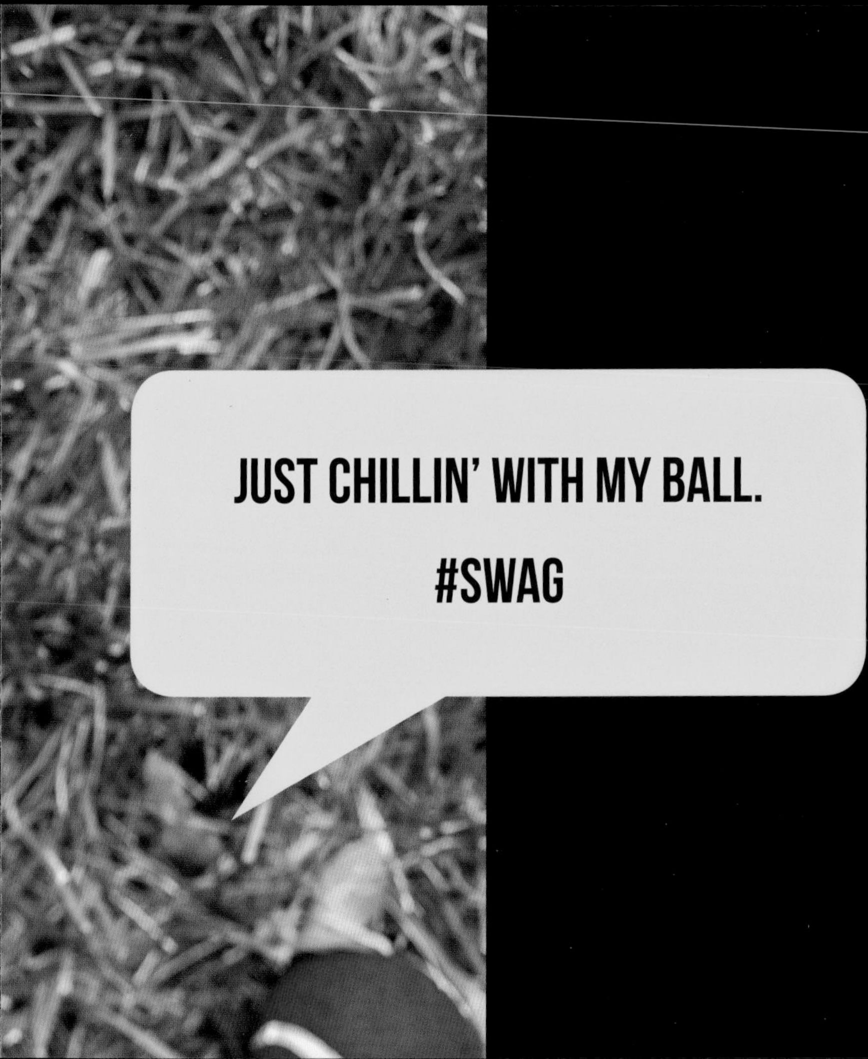
JUST CHILLIN' WITH MY BALL.
#SWAG

DOES THIS ANGLE MAKE MY EARS LOOK BIG?

#SUNSOUT
#TONGUESOUT

NAME: WILF

AGE: 3 YEARS

LIKES: SQUEAKY BALLS, SALMON AND ICE CREAM

DISLIKES: WATER AND ANYONE WHO WON'T THROW HIS SQUEAKY BALL FOR HIM

#SUPERSMILEY

WORKING HARD ON MY TAN.

NAME: JETHRO TULL VOM TEUFELSJOCH

AGE: 3

LIKES: CATCHING THE FRISBEE, HERDING HORSES AND COWS, SNOWBALL FIGHTS AND TAKING THE OCCASIONAL SELFIE!

NAME: BUDDY STOREY

LIKES: MUDDY PUDDLES, BIG STICKS AND TWEETING

TWITTER: @BUDDYPORTSMOUTH

#PHOTOBOMB

PHOTO CREDITS

P.5 NORM © JEREMY VEACH
P.6 PRINCE © SAM BROOKS
P.9 MEG FISK © MADDIE AND EMMA FISK
P.10 © ANNETTE SHAFF
P.13 LUCY © KATHRYN WALLACE YEATON
P.14 MARY © STEWART FERRIS
P.17 FRODO © JULES DELLAERT
P.18 BAILEY © IAN BROWN
P.21 © CATHY KEIFER
P.22 IGGY PUP © ALLYSON BETTRIDGE
P.25 MANI LAYA © ALI GOULDING
P.26 © PAUL MATTHEW PHOTOGRAPHY
P.29 BEAR © JO SPERRING
P.30 © JAVIER BROSCH
P.33 HULA © FAYE HARVEY
P.34 COMMISSARIO COLUMBEAU 'BEAU' FORBES © LAURA AND ALEX FORBES
P.37 © BILDAGENTUR ZOONAR GMBH
P.38 LOTTIE © LINZI HOWSON
RAFA © LIAT JOSHI
P.41, SIR SAMSON © LAURA CIARDIELLIO
P.42 PEPE LE PUG © SARAH REEVES
P.45 BRUNO © JOANNE BEAN
P.46 CHARLIE © VAL RAYNER

P.49 OTTO GARSED-MILLEN © DAVID ANTHONY GERARD GARSED-BENNET JUNIOR
P.50 BUDDY AND PACO © LUIS VIDAL (LOIS)
P.53 LILLY © JUDY WILKINS
P.54 ABIGAIL AND JACK © DYLAN MURPHY
P.57 © BILDAGENTUR ZOONAR GMBH
P.58 BARNEY © LAURA GRAHAM
P.60 © LITTLE MOON
P.62 GIRLIE TAN © GEORGETTE TAN
LEXXI © NANCY COCHRANE
BAMBAM © MAGS
© SHUTTERSTOCK
P.65 © JAVIER BROSCH
P.66 © ALEXANDER BARK
P.69 © MICHAL NOWOSIELSKI
P.70 BRAMBLE © JODIE FORBES
BOB © PHIL GILBERT
P.73 TREHO © GERALDINE VAN DER WESTHUIZEN
P.74 TEDDY © KATHRYN WALLACE YEATON
P.77 VIKI © MARTIN ŠTOURAČ
P.79 SLEITTER © CHRISTAL ALDA
P.80 WILF © JANE HARRINGTON
P.82 © ANNETTE SHAFF
P.84 BONNIE © SANDRA
P.87 JETHRO TULL VOM TEUFELSJOCH © PIA VASCER
P.89 BUDDY STOREY © HALEY STOREY
P.91 KASHA AND LILA © EMMA FERNANDEZ